Tim de Neef

Patricia Cornelius is a founding member of Melbourne Workers Theatre and an award-winning playwright. She has written over twenty plays including *Love, Do Not Go Gentle ...*, *Cunning* (with Irine Vela), *Lilly and May, Jack's Daughters, OPA—A Sexual Odyssey, Max, Platform, Hogs Hairs* and *Leeches*. *Who's Afraid of the Working Class?* and *Fever* were written in collaboration with Andrew Bovell, Melissa Reeves, Christos Tsiolkas and Irine Vela. Her first novel, *My Sister Jill*, was published in 2002.

Morris Gleitzman's brilliantly comic style has endeared him to children and adults alike, and he is now one of Australia's most successful authors. His bestselling books include *Two Weeks with the Queen, Toad Rage, Toad Heaven* and *Toad Away, Girl Underground* and *Once*.

Ashwin Gore as Jamal in the 2005 atyp production.
(Photo: Giselle Haber)

BOY
OVERBOARD

THE PLAY

ADAPTED BY PATRICIA CORNELIUS

FROM THE NOVEL BY MORRIS GLEITZMAN

Currency Press
Sydney

CURRENCY TEENAGE SERIES
First published in 2007
by Currency Press Pty Ltd,
PO Box 2287, Strawberry Hills, NSW, 2012, Australia.
enquiries@currency.com.au
www.currency.com.au

Reprinted in 2009, 2011, 2012, 2013, 2014 (twice), 2015, 2016, 2017, 2018, 2020, 2021

NATIONAL LIBRARY OF AUSTRALIA CIP DATA
Cornelius, Patricia.
Boy overboard: the play.
Includes index.
For upper primary, lower secondary school aged children.
ISBN 978 0 86819 807 1 (pk.).
1. Refugees – Afghanistan – Juvenile drama. 2. Refugees – Australia – Drama.
I. Gleitzman, Morris, 1953–. Boy overboard. II. Title.
A822.33
Typeset for Currency Press by Dean Nottle.
Cover design by Kate Florance, Currency Press.

Publication of this title was assisted by the Commonwealth Government through the Australia Council, its arts funding and advisory body.

Australian Government

Contents

COVER PHOTOGRAPHS

Front cover: (clockwise from far left) Emily Edmondson, Sarah Armanious, Ashwin Gore, Leigh Scully, Alice Workman, Paul Hee, James Pike, Grace Partridge, Lloyd Ruz, Bella Partridge and Johnny Lieu.

Back cover: (back row, left to right) Ashwin Gore and Emily Edmondson (front row, left to right) Leigh Scully, Andrew Gray, Sorie Bangura and Paul Hee. Photos from the 2005 atyp production of *Boy Overboard*.

Photographer: Giselle Haber

Currency Press acknowledges the Traditional Owners of the Country on which we live and work. We pay our respects to all Aboriginal and Torres Strait Islander Elders, past and present.

First Production

Boy Overboard was produced by Australian Theatre for Young People (atyp) at Riverside Theatres, Parramatta, on 19 July 2005, with the following cast:

Rashida	Sarah Armanious
Driver	Sorie Bangura
Mohammed	Julian Dibley-Hall
Bibi	Emily Edmonds
Fatima	Aimee Falzon
Jamal	Ashwin Gore
Aziz / Ensemble	Andrew Gray
Gavin / Mussa / Ensemble	Paul He
Yusuf	Johnny Lieu
Ensemble	Bella Partridge
Ensemble	Grace Partridge
Omar	James Pike
Zoltan / Ensemble	Lloyd Ruz
Andrew	Leigh Scully
Ensemble	Alice Workman

Directors, Timothy Jones and Becky Chapman
Assistant Director, Laura Scrivano
Set and Costume Designer, Genevieve Dugard
Lighting Designer, Luiz Pampolha
Sound Designer, Composer, Max Lambert

Characters

Jamal
Bibi
Fatima, their mother
Mohammed, their father
Yusuf
Zoltan, soccer boy
Mussa, soccer boy
Aziz, soccer boy
Soccer girls
Omar
Rashida
Driver
Gavin
Sailor
Smuggler
Andrew
Chorus of refugees

Setting

A series of platforms at different heights, some suspended, some roped off, create various spaces for the action. One platform is the family house, one a shop, one a block of seating at a stadium; one is the back of a truck littered in sacks under which the family hide. One serves as the docks, one the deck of a boat. They can be moved in and out and around the performance space to accommodate the action. The platforms are like rafts—isolated, floating and vulnerable. There is a boot of a car which is either attached to a car or not. There is also an expanse of tents.

Scene 1

MOHAMMED emerges silently from the shadows and walks to the boot of his taxi. He looks around. Assured he has not been seen, he opens the boot. Three GIRLS, heavily veiled, carrying school books under their arms, quickly get out of the boot. MOHAMMED closes the boot. He watches the GIRLS exit. He furtively looks around. He opens the boot again and another three heavily veiled GIRLS emerge and follow the others. MOHAMMED closes the boot, looks about, opens the boot once more and three more GIRLS climb out and exit.

The sound of drumming feet causes MOHAMMED to panic. He slams the boot shut and runs to the front of the car to drive away.

Darkness. The sound of drumming feet continues—a slightly ominous sound.

'Zeir Baghali', from 'Inside Afghanistan', a recording by Deben Bhattacharya, accompanies the drumming, and continues into the next scene.

Scene 2

The feet belong to a line-up of BOYS. Like a chorus line they move in a choreographed movement sequence toward the audience. It is as if they are playing soccer but there is no ball. The soccer moves are slightly stylised making them dance-like. The ball is so acutely imagined we can almost see it as it bounces from knee to knee to head to foot to knee to chest. The drumming comes to a stop.

The sound of a single bounce of an actual soccer ball is heard. The BOYS listen intently. Again there is the sound of the bouncing ball. They listen and the sound continues.

The line splits to reveal JAMAL behind them, soccer ball in hand, his face lit up in an exuberant smile. The BOYS collectively gasp. JAMAL lifts the ball above his head as if it's some precious thing and moves forward to join the chorus line. They cannot take their eyes off it. YUSUF, JAMAL's one-legged friend, appears on crutches and joins the line.

JAMAL throws the ball high up into the air and a highly stylised game begins. The BOYS move into action and freeze the moment the ball drops and JAMAL stills it with his foot. He narrates the game with intensity.

Jamal Latching onto a fumbled ball from the opposition Manchester United, always in command, in fact, in inspirational form, deliver a stunning, curling, long-distance strike. It's intercepted by Newcastle United and could prove to be an expensive miss but Jamal dramatically, almost miraculously, regains possession and piles on the pressure. Aziz from Newcastle United lunges at me. I dodge the tackle. Aziz is small but he's fast and he comes back for a second lunge.

> *Three young boys, MUSSA, AZIZ and ZOLTAN, engage closely in the game. AZIZ makes a move.*

Aziz You're dead meat, Jamal.

Jamal I dazzle him with my footwork.

> *He does.*

Aziz Too good.

Jamal I weave one way, then the other. The ball at my feet is a blur. Mussa, who's also Newcastle United, tries to remove my feet from my ankles.

> *MUSSA moves into stylised action.*

Mussa You're finished, Jamal.

Jamal I avoid his big boots and flick the ball between his legs.

Mussa You always do that!

Jamal [*with a laugh*] I duck past him, steer the ball around a bomb crater, and find myself in front of goal. And there's Yusuf.

> *YUSUF, in position as if between goalposts, balances on his one foot, his crutches stretched out to the sides.*

Yusuf the terrible.

> *YUSUF lets out an almighty growl.*

His eyes never leave the ball at my toes.

Yusuf Don't even think about it, Jamal.

ZOLTAN gestures to JAMAL to pass.

Zoltan Over here, Jamal.

Jamal That's Zoltan, he's Manchester United with me.

Zoltan Pass.

Jamal Normally I would. I'm known for it. Ask anyone.

Zoltan Jamal's a good dribbler.

Aziz He is. He's a brilliant passer.

Mussa He's fantastic at dribbling and passing.

Jamal If I had an unexploded shell for every goal I've set up I could go into the scrap metal business.

Yusuf It's true, he'd be a rich man,

Jamal Just once I want to score myself.

Zoltan Jamal, over here!

Jamal I want to smack the ball with all my strength and watch it whiz past Yusuf like a Scud missile.

Zoltan Here, Jamal. Here!

Jamal All I've got to do is get around Yusuf.

Mussa Not a chance, Jamal.

Aziz Not a chance.

Jamal He's really good at diving saves, especially for a kid with one leg.

YUSUF growls.

I really should pass. I steady myself... and shoot.

The boys watch the progress of JAMAL's imagined shot. Their faces register pain or pleasure as it clearly misses.

Aziz Weak.

MUSSA laughs.

Yusuf Very sad, Jamal, very sad.

Zoltan [*indignant*] Jamal, I was unmarked.

Jamal [*to ZOLTAN*] Sorry. [*To the audience*] I wait for Aziz and Mussa to say something nasty about mid-field players who think they're strikers, but aren't.

The boys are silent but stare ahead in shock. JAMAL talks on, oblivious to them.

But they're good friends, they forgive me.

Aziz Jamal.

Jamal They understand that every now and then you've just got to go for it.

Mussa Jamal.

Jamal Because one day, I'll take a shot and it will roar through those goalposts.

Zoltan Jamal!

Jamal What!

He looks at their faces and realises something is up.

Is it the government?

The lights come up on nine-year-old BIBI, her hands defiantly placed on her hips, her veil slipped off her head. She has managed to retrieve the soccer ball and it now lies at her feet.

[*In horror*] Bibi.

Boys Your sister.

Silence.

Bibi [*in a formidable voice*] I want to play.

Together JAMAL and the boys take a step back.

I want to play.

Jamal Go home.

Yusuf Go away.

Mussa Not a chance.

Aziz You can't.

Zoltan No way.

Bibi I'm sick of being stuck indoors.

Zoltan [*to JAMAL*] Do something. She's your sister.

Bibi I want to play soccer.

Again JAMAL and the boys take a step back.

[*Pushing the ball with her toe*] Come on, you soft lumps of camel poop, tackle me.

Jamal Go home.

Mussa Go.

Aziz You can't play.

Zoltan No way.

Bibi Why? Are you afraid you won't get your ball back?

Pause. JAMAL takes up the challenge.

Jamal Tackle her.

The boys respond to the challenge. One at a time they move. Deftly BIBI sidesteps AZIZ, then ZOLTAN, weaves past MUSSA, and flicks the ball between JAMAL's legs. She stops and faces them triumphantly.

You promised you'd only play soccer in your bedroom.

BIBI turns and the lights come up on YUSUF at the goals. He growls. BIBI growls in return. ZOLTAN moves to the side of her.

Zoltan Bibi, over here. Pass.

AZIZ moves to the other side.

Aziz Me, Bibi, pass it to me.

BIBI ignores them and shoots. YUSUF dives but the ball scuds past his fingers, through the goalposts and disappears over a mound. Despite themselves, the boys lift their arms exultantly.

Boys Yes!

BIBI turns and faces them.

Bibi Goal for Afghanistan!

Silence.

AZIZ, MUSSA and ZOLTAN remember the real world and that BIBI is a girl.

Aziz Cover yourself.

Zoltan You should be ashamed.

Mussa   Go indoors immediately.

>   *BIBI growls furiously. JAMAL is uncomfortable but defends his sister.*

Jamal   You've got to admit it was a good goal.
Bibi   [*running off after the ball*] I'll get the ball.
Jamal   No, Bibi. Wait!

>   *JAMAL pulls YUSUF to his feet and they chase after her. The boys exit.*

Scene 3

BIBI runs onto the stage. She stops when she sees the soccer ball ahead.

Bibi   I can dribble better, I can pass better, and I can shoot better. I should be playing soccer every day.

>   *She walks towards the ball and suddenly stops. She slowly looks down at her feet. She whimpers softly. She has stood on a landmine. She remains very still. Slowly she lifts her head and lets out a terrible scream.*

>   *JAMAL and YUSUF appear in a rush.*

Jamal   Bibi!

>   *JAMAL and YUSUF know immediately what BIBI has done.*

Jamal & Yusuf   [*together*] Oh, no.

>   *They pull up quickly. BIBI whimpers pitifully.*

Jamal   Hang on, Bibi, it's going to be okay.
Yusuf   Please, Allah, don't let her legs be blown off. Not even just one.
Jamal   Bibi, don't move. If you lift your weight off the metal plate it'll explode.
Bibi   [*whimpering*] I know.
Jamal   The mines are supposed to be cleared this close to the village.
Yusuf   [*looking at his one leg*] That's what they said seven years ago.
Bibi   What are we going to do?

6

Jamal I know this looks bad, no, this is bad, like if we were playing soccer and the other team was a goal ahead, perhaps even two, and there was only a minute left of play. The secret is, never give up, even when things are looking hopeless.

BIBI bursts into tears.

Bibi Don't say hopeless, you camel poop!

JAMAL and YUSUF talk together.

Jamal Wait with Bibi while I go get someone.

Yusuf Wait. If people come to rescue Bibi, they'll see she's a girl and that she's out here and she'll be in as much trouble as she is now.

Jamal There's only one thing to do.

JAMAL walks towards BIBI treading extremely carefully as he goes. YUSUF follows further behind, walking in JAMAL's footsteps.

Bibi What are you doing, Jamal? Don't come any closer, you'll be blown up.

They reach BIBI. JAMAL puts his foot next to hers.

Jamal Okay, slide your foot off the metal plate while I slide my foot on.

BIBI is aghast.

Yusuf [*whispering*] If that plate pops up ...

Jamal Bibi, slide your foot off slowly.

Bibi But then you'll be on the mine. You could be blown up.

Jamal It's probably a dud. A lot of these landmines are twenty years old and totally clapped out. Aren't they, Yusuf?

YUSUF looks down at his missing leg. BIBI follows his eyes. She cries.

Bibi No! It's too risky.

Jamal Bibi, if you get blown up, people will find out you've been playing soccer.

Bibi Mum and Dad are always doing things they're not meant to do.

Jamal [*more anxious*] Bibi, if the government finds out a girl's been playing soccer, Mum and Dad are in big trouble.

BIBI thinks for a moment.

Bibi [*angrily*] I don't want to get blown up and I don't want you to get blown up either. It's not fair.

Yusuf [*alarmed*] Don't stamp your feet. Whatever you do, don't stamp your feet.

JAMAL tries to placate her.

Jamal Let me step on the mine. Then Yusuf will help you get home. Then he will get someone to come back and help me. We'll all be fine.

Yusuf We'll all be fine.

BIBI glares for a long time.

Bibi Okay, but if I die, I hope you do too! Because if I'm dead and you aren't I'd really miss you.

Jamal Here goes.

YUSUF holds BIBI's feet as she shuffles off the mine and JAMAL shuffles on. BIBI hugs JAMAL.

Okay, run for it.

YUSUF grabs his crutches and takes off. BIBI continues to hug her brother.

Bibi Jamal, is it all right if I keep on playing soccer?

Jamal Yes, Bibi.

BIBI follows YUSUF but turns one last time.

Bibi But if you're dead I wouldn't feel like it.

Jamal Thanks, Bibi.

BIBI follows YUSUF offstage.

JAMAL, alone now, fully realises the misery of his situation.

[*Quietly*] Don't tremble, Jamal, whatever you do, don't tremble. I ask the fierce, brave desert warriors of Mum's family to give me strength. Please, don't tremble. I ask the honest and hard-working bakers of my dad's family to give me patience to wait for Yusuf to bring someone to help me.

JAMAL's litany is interrupted by the appearance of BIBI.

Bibi Jamal!

She runs frantically towards JAMAL.

I can't. I don't want to leave you.

She flings her arms around JAMAL and buries her face in his chest. They teeter there for a moment and finally fall, off the mine.

They scream one almighty scream. Silence.

They lie perfectly still for a while until, lifting their heads, they look towards the mine in disbelief. BIBI angrily gets up.

I'd like to kick you in the guts.

She pulls back her leg to do just that.

Jamal No! Come on, we've got to get you home before our luck runs out.

They exit.

Scene 4

YUSUF enters in great strides on his crutches. He looks around him to see if it's clear, and signals with a whistle and one crutch held high in the air.

Yusuf All clear.

JAMAL and BIBI tentatively enter. BIBI has her skirt tucked in and wears YUSUF's hat and JAMAL's jacket.

Jamal [*to BIBI*] Keep low.

The sound of a truck roars by.

Yusuf Watch out!

YUSUF and JAMAL leap back and hit the deck. BIBI stands her ground. She picks up a rock and hurtles it at the departing truck.

Jamal Bibi, stop!

Her hands on her hips, BIBI is defiant.

Bibi I hate trucks!

Yusuf Keep your voice down, you're meant to be a boy.

Bibi I don't care if I'm meant to be a goat.

Jamal We don't want to draw attention to ourselves.

Bibi Trucks took Anisa's dad away and he's never come back.

Yusuf [*struggling to get up*] A truck will take you away too, Bibi, if you keep throwing rocks at it.

Bibi I hate this country.

The boys, in a panic, look around hoping that BIBI hasn't been overheard.

Jamal Ssh, Bibi. You love our country.

Bibi It's camel snot.

Yusuf Ssh, Bibi. It is not.

Bibi It's a bum boil.

YUSUF falls off his crutches in shock.

Jamal If we won the World Cup, you'd love your country then.

Yusuf Everybody'd love us then. Other nations would respect us and stop bombing us all the time.

Bibi I bet Manchester hasn't got landmines.

Jamal They might have a few.

Yusuf Not unless they were put there by Arsenal supporters.

Jamal We should be grateful. Our house has still got a roof. Our mum and dad are alive. We've still got our arms and legs.

JAMAL immediately realises what he has said and he and BIBI look apologetically at YUSUF.

Yusuf [*indignantly*] My house has still got a roof.

Jamal We need to get our story straight before we get home.

Bibi How about we've been looking for Anisa's lost cat?

Jamal How about we had to carry Yusuf's grandfather to the doctor?

Yusuf Why? My grandfather has both his legs. He can walk.

JAMAL playfully slaps the back of YUSUF's head.

Bibi Then we have been doing something good and we won't be in so much trouble.

Jamal Right, we carried Yusuf's grandfather to the doctor. He was very sick.

Yusuf They won't believe you. My grandfather weighs a ton.

The roar of another truck resounds.

Jamal Quick, duck.

JAMAL and YUSUF run for cover. BIBI bends to pick up a rock but JAMAL comes back.

Oh, no you don't.

He pulls her away.

Scene 5

FATIMA stands on a platform before a pile of books. She picks up a book and begins to tear it up. She stops suddenly and looks closely at one of the pages.

Fatima Our history is a tragedy—a difficult lesson to teach. We have never not been at war, and it has devastated us.

She looks up. Three veiled GIRLS appear on a platform.

Girl 1 So many invaders, it was hard to remember all the names.

Girl 2 First it was the Achaemenids from Persia, then it was Alexander the Great, then the Parthians and the Saka and the Mauryan rulers.

Girl 3 Then the Kushan from China. They were conquered by Persia.

Girl 2 Then Eastern India took over.

Girl 1 Next there were invaders from the Arabian Peninsula.

Girl 3 Islamic dynasties ruled until the infamous Genghis Khan brought the Mongols…

Girl 2 Who plundered the cities and massacred the people.

Girl 1 Then came, Timur.

Girl 2 Then Zahir-ud-Din Muhammad took Kabul.

Girl 3 Then the Moghuls.

Girl 1 The Safavids from Persia.

Girl 2 The Uzbek from Uzbekistan.

Girl 1 Then the British and Indian armies invaded Afghanistan.

Fatima And not so long ago, in 1979, the Soviet Union invaded. [*She rips the pages, then picks up another book.*] The wonders of Afghanistan are the most delightful, and heart-breaking lessons of all.

Girl 3 The Dam of Awe, the Hot Springs of Obey.

Girl 1 The curious enigma of the sixty-five-metre tall Minaret of Jam.

Girl 2 The beautiful Blue Mosque in Mazar-e Sharif.

Fatima The extraordinary Buddhas of Bamiyam, now destroyed by the Taliban. A vast and marvellous land is Afghanistan.

> *She rips up the pages, then picks up another book. She rips pages at various intervals as she speaks.*

Girl 2 Afghanistan is rich in oil and gems.

Girl 1 It has magnificent mountain ranges.

Girl 3 Vast and mysterious deserts.

Girl 1 Green valleys that grow the most luscious fruit.

Fatima But my girls have never been free to go further than their village and have tasted only the local yams. Afghanistan is reduced to fields of landmines. [*She picks up another book. She rips.*] Our brilliant poets have inspired the world with words of such beauty and power. And we are left with a government who will not allow our girls to learn.

> *The GIRLS fade.*

I'm sorry, girls, there will be no more class. The government knows about the school.

> *MOHAMMED enters holding a long spade-like tool. A loaf of bread (a naan) sits on it. He picks the bread up in his hands.*

Mohammed If we had time I would stuff it with potatoes and leeks. Smell it. Mmm, smell it.

Fatima There's no other smell like it.

Mohammed No better. This oven has baked a million loaves. My father, my grandfather, my great-grandfather, my—

Fatima I know, my love, I know.

MOHAMMED breaks the bread in two.

Mohammed My last loaf. My very last.

He breaks off a piece and gives it to FATIMA. He bites into a piece.

I will never make bread that tastes this good again.

Julian Dibley-Hall (front) as Mohammed and Aimée Falzon as Fatima in the 2005 atyp production. (Photo: Giselle Haber)

Scene 6

JAMAL and BIBI are outside the door of their house. JAMAL is taking his jacket off BIBI while she puts on her veil.

Jamal Whatever you do, don't mention soccer.
Bibi No soccer. [*She points to the ball.*] How are you going to explain that?

> *JAMAL puts the ball by the door and covers it with his jacket.*
>
> *They enter the house.*
>
> *MOHAMMED and FATIMA are surrounded by suitcases and bags. JAMAL and BIBI brace themselves for a dressing-down. Instead their parents rush to embrace them.*

Fatima Jamal and Bibi, you know we love you very much.
Jamal Yes.
Bibi Yes.
Mohammed You know you two are the most precious things in our lives.
Jamal Yes.
Bibi Yes.
Mohammed We've got to leave.
Jamal What?
Bibi What?
Fatima We've got to leave.
Mohammed And we can't ever come back.
Jamal No.
Bibi No.
Jamal We don't have to leave. Nobody saw Bibi playing soccer.
Bibi The landmine didn't even go off.
Fatima What?
Jamal Why do we have to leave? Is it because the brake lights don't work on the taxi?
Mohammed It's more serious than that.

Jamal You only bought that petrol from the army once.

Bibi It's impossible to be a taxi driver without petrol.

Fatima The government has found out about the school.

> *Silence.*

Jamal How did they find out?

Mohammed Perhaps someone saw the girls getting into the boot of the taxi when I picked them up.

Fatima We haven't much time.

Mohammed We will leave at first light.

Bibi I don't want to go.

Jamal I don't want to go either.

Fatima They will find out who is involved with the school and they will arrest us one by one.

Bibi [*full of bravado*] If they come around here, they'll get a faceful of rocks.

> *FATIMA hugs BIBI.*

[*In a tiny voice*] Mum, I'm scared.

Jamal So am I.

> *FATIMA takes something wrapped in a cloth from one of the bags. She unwraps it. It is an ancient candlestick embedded with precious stones.*

Fatima Our candlestick has been in my family for hundreds of years. My ancestors would burn a candle before they went into battle. With this candle nothing will happen to us. Remember how the candle burned through the air raids and kept us safe?

> *They look at the candlestick hopefully.*

Scene 7

In the middle of the night, the moonlight shines brightly on a deserted street. The door to the family house opens and FATIMA and MOHAMMED sneak out and disappear into the shadows. Moments later, JAMAL slips quietly outside. He carries his soccer ball. He stops in the middle of the street and sits on his ball. He is thinking very hard. Suddenly an idea comes to him and he rises to his feet. He looks down at his ball.

Jamal [*excitedly, but in a whisper*] Yes.

> *He drops the ball off his foot onto the knee, back onto the foot. He stops. He punctuates his sentences with some very fancy footwork.*

It's a match to set the heart racing. As predicted, Manchester United have the overwhelming possession of the ball, but they are met with an impregnable series of defensive walls with super-tight man to man marking from the players from ... Af-ghan-i-stan. A soaring ball comes into the six-yard area and Manchester United's goalkeeper is woefully out of position and there is ... Jamal, to head home. Manchester's usually inspired substitutions fail to ignite the side and Afghanistan, unbelievably, are the European Champions.

> *JAMAL lifts his arms and imagines he hears the roar of a crowd. And he does, ZOLTAN, AZIZ, MUSSA and YUSUF, with two legs, appear dressed in Afghani national colour soccer uniforms. JAMAL does not look at them when he addresses them; they are in his dream.*

Yusuf, you've got two legs.
Yusuf They insist on two legs to join the national soccer team. Besides, I'm in your dream.
Jamal We'll win the World Cup and the government will be proud.
Zoltan We'll be popular.
Aziz We'll never be threatened ...
Mussa Or bullied ...
Yusuf Or killed.
Jamal It's a good plan. A really good plan.

> *BIBI and three other GIRLS enter dressed in soccer uniforms.*

Bibi [*formidable*] I want to play.

Girl 1 So do I.
Girl 2 And I.
Girl 3 And me too.

>   *Pause. The other boys look doubtful.*

Jamal Why not? We can do it. We'll improve our skills and impress the government. We'll start a national team and win the hearts of the people of Afghanistan. The government will forgive Mum and Dad. And we won't have to leave because how could they stay mad at the best player of the Afghanistan national soccer team.

>   *The team chants, 'Afghanistan, Afghanistan, Afghanistan'.*

The celebration of the Afghani team was nothing less than extravagant.

>   *JAMAL lifts his top over his head and runs in a circle.*

>   *The chant fades as do the members of the team as they disappear into the night.*

>   *BIBI comes through the door, in usual dress, carrying the candlestick to light her way. She interrupts JAMAL's reverie.*

Bibi Jamal, what are you doing?
Jamal [*his head still covered*] What?
Bibi You're playing soccer in the street.
Jamal [*pulling his head free*] What? Bibi. You should be asleep.
Bibi I want to play.
Jamal It's late, go to bed before Mum and Dad catch you.
Bibi I want to play.
Jamal You need to sleep, we've a big day ahead of us.

>   *BIBI puts down the candlestick and quickly sneaks the ball from JAMAL's feet.*

Bibi Come on, get it from me.

>   *JAMAL lunges at her but she flips the ball over his ankle, runs around the other side of him and traps it under her foot.*

Penalty shot.

BIBI steps back, runs at the ball and boots it in the direction of their house.

There is a huge explosion. The children almost vanish in a cloud of dust.

Scene 8

Out on the road.

YUSUF enters, racing on his crutches. He checks to see if it is clear and whistles. JAMAL, with the candlestick under his arm, pulls BIBI onto the road.

Yusuf Hurry, you've got to get as far away as possible. They might come back.
Bibi Stop, Jamal, stop.
Jamal We've got to keep going, Bibi.
Bibi I can't. I've got to stop.
Yusuf It's not safe.
Jamal Yusuf, where will we go?
Yusuf I don't know, but if they catch you—
Bibi Please, can we rest for a bit?

> *JAMAL stops and he and BIBI sit, the candlestick between them. YUSUF keeps a nervous lookout.*

I'm afraid.
Jamal Me too.
Bibi Mum and Dad—
Jamal Ssh, Bibi, ssh.

> *The three of them are silent and bow their heads in sadness. Slowly, almost unconsciously, JAMAL and BIBI put out their hands to touch the candlestick.*

> *The lights of a car pick them up. JAMAL pulls BIBI up to make a run for it. YUSUF follows but looks back. His face is caught in the lights and it is jubilant.*

Yusuf Hey! Jamal, Bibi, come back.

*The children return. MOHAMMED appears. He sneaks around the
taxi and calls from the boot.*

Mohammed Bibi! Jamal! Thank God!

*The children run to their father. They hug silently for some time.
YUSUF exits at great speed.*

Jamal They blew up our house.

Bibi We thought you were inside.

Jamal Asleep in your bed.

Bibi We thought…

Mohammed Hopefully the authorities think so too. It will give us
more time. Come, we must go. [*He throws open the boot.*] Quickly,
get in.

Bibi Where's Mum? Dad? Where's Mum?

Mohammed It's okay. Mum will meet us tomorrow.

Jamal [*terrified*] Where is she?

Mohammed Would I lie to you? She'll meet us tomorrow, I promise
you. Now quickly get in.

He lifts BIBI into the boot. She has the candlestick in her hand.

Your mother's ancestors have kept us extra safe tonight.

*JAMAL looks around for YUSUF. He shrugs sadly and is about to
get into the boot when YUSUF enters on his crutches. He has a
soccer ball tucked under his arm.*

Yusuf Jamal!

MOHAMMED disappears towards the front of the car.

Where will you go?

Jamal I don't know.

Yusuf Will you be back?

Jamal I have a plan. I'm going to change the world.

Yusuf [*offering him the soccer ball*] You'll need this, then.

Jamal I can't take your soccer ball.

Yusuf I want it back when you've changed the world.

Jamal Thank you, Yusuf. I'll miss you.

YUSUF and JAMAL hug. JAMAL climbs into the boot. YUSUF goes to close it but stops and opens it again.

Yusuf Jamal, if you get the chance, send me a leg.

He closes the boot.

Scene 9

Daylight.

MOHAMMED opens the boot of the taxi and the two weary children appear. They are outside an abandoned shop which leans against an enormous curved wall. Above them are straggling bunches of tangled cassette tape hanging off light poles.

Mohammed Good morning, you two.
Jamal Is Mum here?
Mohammed Not yet. She will be, a bit later.
Bibi How much later?

Pause. MOHAMMED is clearly distressed by the questions.

Mohammed I'm not sure exactly when she'll be here.
Jamal Why not?
Bibi Where is she?
Mohammed I promise you, she'll be here.

For a moment the children remain doubtful but finally they accept his promise. JAMAL looks up at the tape hanging above them.

Tape trees. Tapes are taken from motorists and chucked up on the lines as a warning. This government hates music. [*He musses JAMAL's hair.*] That's why I taught you to whistle.

MOHAMMED enters the shop and the children follow.

Come on, let's get you two settled. You'll be safe here until I get back.
Jamal Are you leaving us here?
Bibi You're not.
Mohammed I've got to pick Mum up.

Jamal We'll go with you.

Mohammed It's better if you wait here.

Bibi Why?

> *MOHAMMED drops his head. He doesn't answer.*

Mohammed I won't be long.

> *He kisses BIBI on the head and goes outside, taking JAMAL with him. He hands JAMAL a wad of money.*

This is in case I'm not back by this afternoon. Find a taxi and give the money to the driver. He'll take you back to the village. I'll be back, I promise.

> *He kisses JAMAL on the head. JAMAL is transfixed by the money in his hand. He waves but when he looks up his father has gone. He returns to BIBI who has been listening at the door.*

Bibi If Dad doesn't come back we're going to use that money to buy a tank and blow someone up.

> *She tries to stay brave but finally bursts into tears. JAMAL hugs her.*

We'll be together again, won't we?

Jamal Yes, whatever happens, this family will always be together. We may not be in Manchester, but we will always be united.

> *BIBI lifts her head from JAMAL's shoulder and frowns at his bad joke. She gives him a light punch on the arm for it.*
>
> *JAMAL pulls out the candlestick from a bag and lights the candle.*

There. Now they'll be safe. Can you feel it, Bibi? Our ancestors are looking after us.

> *There's a barely audible sound.*

Bibi Jamal, I think I can hear them.

> *Again the sound.*

Jamal [*in disbelief*] So can I.

They follow the sound outside and look up at the huge curved wall that towers above them. Once more there is the distant roar of a crowd.

Do you know what this is?

Bibi No.

Jamal It's a stadium. A soccer stadium. We're going home, Bibi.

Bibi Are we?

Jamal This is all fitting into my plan.

Bibi What plan?

Jamal To form a national soccer team for Afghanistan.

Bibi I want to play.

Jamal With your skills, I have no doubt you'll be in the team.

Bibi Hurray!

Jamal Behind that wall is our safety. There will be soccer officials on the look-out for talent like ours. Come on, we're about to save the day.

They exit.

Scene 10

A rack of wooden seating faces the audience. A row of identically turbaned MEN look most severe as they sit in the same position, their hands on their knees, staring out. Collectively they sound a single, ominous note.

A light picks up the faces of JAMAL and BIBI who have climbed in under the seats.

'Battle Tune', from 'Inside Afghanistan', a recording by Deben Bhattacharya, accompanies the scene.

Jamal There must be a match. This is great, Bibi, the national team selectors will be here.

Bibi I don't think I'm ready for national selectors. I've only ever scored one goal.

Jamal It's talent they're looking for in an eleven-year-old, not experience.

The turbaned MEN repeat the note.

Perhaps it's a big match. A famous club on tour, Real Madrid or Juventas. What if it's Manchester United?

BIBI has become aware of something that JAMAL is determined to ignore.

Bibi Jamal.

Jamal Sir Alex Ferguson could be in the dressing room right now.

Bibi Jamal.

Jamal Giving his players a stirring speech. Checking their hamstrings.

Bibi [*more insistent*] Jamal, look. Look.

The note is repeated. JAMAL looks. Again the note is sung.

What's going on, Jamal? Why are there trucks on the field?

Jamal And soldiers.

Bibi They're dragging some women out.

Jamal Their hands are tied.

Bibi The soldiers have guns.

The note sounds.

They're making the women kneel down?

Jamal Let's go, Bibi.

Bibi One of the women is running away.

Jamal I see her.

Bibi She looks familiar.

Jamal I know.

The note sounds.

Bibi Oh, no.

Jamal Oh, no. Come on, Bibi, we've got to go.

Bibi [*screwing up her eyes*] Oh, Jamal.

JAMAL and BIBI cover their eyes with their hands. The sound of the MEN has reached a crescendo and it suddenly stops.

The sound of a shot rings out.

Scene 11

Back at the shop, BIBI and JAMAL kneel on either side of the candlestick. They are extremely distressed.

Jamal We call upon our ancestors, the desert warriors, to keep our mother safe.

Bibi Please bring our mother to us.

Jamal Guide our father so that he may find her.

Bibi And we can all be together again.

Jamal Please.

Bibi Why aren't they here, Jamal?

Jamal I don't know, Bibi, I don't know. Remember, Bibi, the secret of soccer is to never give up, even when things are looking hopeless.

Bibi Don't say hopeless, Jamal, please don't say hopeless.

There is a beep of a car horn. The children rush outside to find MOHAMMED. They hug him close.

Jamal Where's Mum?

Bibi Where is she, Dad?

MOHAMMED moves to the boot of the car. JAMAL and BIBI are so afraid they can barely speak.

Jamal Where's Mum?

Bibi Where is she?

MOHAMMED puts his finger to his lips. He opens the boot and FATIMA sits up. The children embrace her.

Anisa's mum was running, she had her hands tied, they had a gun.

Jamal In the stadium.

A distant roar from the stadium sounds. The family looks toward the wall. FATIMA understands.

Bibi What will happen to Anisa?

Jamal We thought that you—

Fatima I went to the girls' homes to warn their families. Rahme and her family, and Sahar and her daughters had packed up and left. Khadija and Fatim's houses were bombed. I hope they got away. I saw Hamideh and her daughter, Rehab, pulled from their home and forced into a truck. There were others inside—I could hear their prayers. I am sorry, Bibi, Anisa was also there with her mother.

BIBI weeps silently in her mother's arms.

Mohammed We must keep going. We're not safe yet.

He gestures for the children to get in the boot.

Jamal Where are we going?
Fatima A long way away.
Bibi Are we coming back?

FATIMA hesitates and looks sadly at MOHAMMED.

Jamal When are we going?
Mohammed As soon as I sell the taxi and get money for our trip.
Bibi & Jamal [*together*] Sell the taxi!
Mohammed We won't need it where we're going. Quick, time to go.

He lifts BIBI into the boot. He remembers the soccer ball and candlestick and goes to get them. On the way back he stops suddenly and looks up at the stadium wall.

Jamal [*angrily*] I'll play soccer in this stadium one day. Nothing but soccer will be permitted. And it will be filled with people, men and women, who will cheer and be proud of their team.

He turns and gets into the boot of the car and pulls it shut.

Scene 12

Darkness. The sound of a truck fills the silence. Mounds of sacks become visible on the floor. Suddenly BIBI's head pops up.

Bibi Where are we going?

Pause. FATIMA's head appears from under the sacks. BIBI has asked this question many times.

Clockwise from front left : Emily Edmondson as Bibi, Aimée Falzon as Fatima, Julian Dibley-Hall as Mohammed and Ashwin Gore as Jamal in the 2005 atyp production. (Photo: Giselle Haber)

Fatima Bibi, be patient.

They disappear under the sacks. Pause. BIBI re-emerges.

Bibi My knees hurt. Where's this truck taking us?

FATIMA's head comes up.

Fatima You must stay down, Bibi.

They disappear under the sacks. The truck roars on. JAMAL's head pops up.

Jamal Dad, where exactly are we going?

JAMAL's question remains unanswered.

Dad? Hey, Dad, where are we going?

Finally FATIMA emerges from under the sacks.

Fatima We should tell them, Mohammed.

MOHAMMED and BIBI emerge.

Mohammed Mum and I have decided that we should all live as far away as we can.

Fatima We've decided to leave Afghanistan.

JAMAL's jaw drops.

Jamal Leave Afghanistan!

Bibi Where will we go?

Mohammed [*sadly*] A long, long way away.

Jamal Will they play soccer there?

Fatima [*sadly*] We will find a wonderful place to start a new life.

Bibi Where?

Fatima Where people are safe and happy and it's far enough away so the government won't find us.

Jamal Will they play soccer there?

Fatima We will find a place where we will be welcome.

Mohammed Where we will make a better life for us.

Fatima Where we will be safe.

Suddenly the noise of the engine stops and someone shouts.

Mohammed Get down!

> *The four heads drop quickly under the sacks. Silence. BIBI puts her head up.*

Bibi I'm scared.

> *FATIMA quickly emerges and pulls BIBI under. Silence.*

> *There is the sound of someone thumping the side of the truck before the motor starts and they are on their way again. FATIMA and MOHAMMED emerge from the sacks. They stretch out and hold each other's hands.*

> *'Song from Heart', from 'Inside Afghanistan', a recording by Deben Bhattacharya.*

Mohammed & Fatima [*together, sadly*] Goodbye Afghanistan.

Scene 13

A line-up of REFUGEES faces the audience. They are deeply afraid for their loved ones.

Refugees Have you seen my mother? She crossed the border a month before me. I can't find her.

Have you heard anything about my brother? I was to meet him here.

I've had no news from my husband.

I don't know if my father was stopped at the border.

My parents, my wife, my children, I can't find them.

I've been waiting for my son for over six months now.

I don't know where my family are?

Nor I.

Nor I.

I have no idea.

> *Meanwhile hundreds of makeshift tents are erected, strung across an enormous expanse. JAMAL and his family weave their*

way through and finally find a place to sit. JAMAL practises a sequence of ball to head to knee, etc.

A boy with a scowl, OMAR, emerges from behind a tent and spots JAMAL. He takes out a plastic bottle of water.

Omar   Wanna buy some water?

Jamal   No thanks.

Omar   Only fifty cents American.

Jamal   No.

Omar   This isn't washing water, it's drinking water.

Jamal   How long have you been here?

Omar   A year.

Jamal   A year!

Omar   Come on, buy the water, would you?

Jamal   No. [*He indicates the ball.*] But do you want to play?

OMAR nods. JAMAL kicks the ball to him. He picks it up and runs.

Hey!

JAMAL and OMAR enter a stylised chase.

Can't lose that ball. This kid needs a whack around the head. Stop! At least it's good practice, dodging tent pegs, jumping over families. [*To someone on the ground*] Excuse me. Avoiding prayer mats and tethered goats. I'm gaining on him. I don't reckon he even plays soccer, there's not much puff left in him.

JAMAL catches OMAR by the back of his jacket and OMAR strains against his hold.

What do you think you're doing? Give me back my ball.

JAMAL pulls him hard and grabs onto the ball. They both pull with all their strength to gain the ball.

Omar   Why didn't you just buy the water?

Jamal   Without this ball I can't return to Afghanistan.

JAMAL gives an almighty pull and retrieves the ball. Out of breath, they stare at one another angrily.

A groaning, miserable sound fills the camp.

What's that?

Omar What?

Jamal What's that noise?

Omar I can't hear anything.

The groans of misery intensify.

Jamal That?

Omar That? That's just the sound of the camp.

JAMAL is overwhelmed by the sound. It is as if it hurts him.

Get used to it. That's what life here sounds like.

The roar of a truck sounds and JAMAL steps out as two lights appear in front of him.

Hey! Watch out.

JAMAL puts up his arms to flag the truck down. The truck stops and JAMAL stands in the lights. The DRIVER appears from out of the darkness.

Driver Get out of the bloody way!

Jamal Sick people. You've got to get help for them.

Driver Where?

Jamal Over there. Loads of them.

Driver They're sick, they're hungry and they're stuck here. Can't go back and they can't move on.

Jamal How will they get food?

Driver We've been waiting for a week for a shipment of food.

Jamal Will it come soon?

Driver We've been going to the airstrip every day. When they do come we could do with some help. You two fellows want to hand out food?

Omar If you pay enough.

Jamal I will if I'm still here. We might have left Pakistan by then.

Driver Where to?

Jamal I don't know. To some place far away.

Driver [*calling over his shoulder*] Hey, Gav, someone here you should meet.

> *GAVIN appears from the truck.*

Here's someone from far away. Tell them about Australia.

Gavin Best country in the world, Australia.

Omar Where's Australia?

Gavin [*pointing*] That way.

Jamal You're Australian?

Gavin I sure am.

> *The DRIVER tousles GAVIN's blonde hair.*

Driver You don't think he's from around here with this mop of hair, do you?

Jamal Are there any good soccer teams in Australia?

Gavin Some great ones. Where I come from, Dubbo Abattoirs United are world-beaters. They've won the Western District Trophy for the last nine years.

Jamal That's wonderful. Are girls allowed to play soccer in Australia?

Gavin Of course.

Jamal Are women allowed to be teachers?

Gavin Definitely. There are thousands of schools.

Jamal And taxi drivers and bakers?

Gavin Thousands of taxis and cake shops.

Omar Is there enough food for everyone in Australia?

Gavin Buckets. Supermarkets never close. Even better, if you've got a fishing line you can catch your own tea.

Omar Tea out of a bucket sounds very good.

Driver Doesn't it. I think I might come with you.

Jamal So people in Australia are happy?

Gavin They start laughing first thing in the morning and don't stop until two hours after they go to sleep at night.

> *GAVIN laughs and JAMAL joins him exuberantly which makes GAVIN laugh harder and the DRIVER snort with laughter. OMAR, frowning, looks on.*

Driver I'm going to laugh myself sick. Come on, we've got to get this medical equipment delivered.

He makes his way back to the truck.

Jamal Do all Australians speak my language?

Gavin Most Australians have never heard of Afghansitan.

GAVIN goes to leave.

Jamal Do you have mines in Australia?

Gavin Lots of mines, mines everywhere. Full of gold, some of them.

Jamal Gold!

Driver [*calling from the darkness*] Gavin, we've got to hit the road.

Gavin On my way. [*To JAMAL*] Maybe I'll see you in Australia one day.

GAVIN joins the DRIVER and the lights pull back as they reverse and disappear. JAMAL is left in a daze.

Jamal Gold. [*He suddenly smiles.*] If you get your leg blown off, you can afford the hospital bills. Oh, Yusuf, if only you had stood on a mine in Australia. I've got to tell Mum and Dad the good news.

He walks in one direction and stops. He changes direction and again stops. It is dusk and night is descending rapidly.

What sort of desert warrior am I? I can't even find my own way home.

Omar I know the camp like the back of my hand.

Jamal Will you help me get back to my family?

Omar It'll cost you.

Jamal I haven't got any money.

Omar The ball.

JAMAL pauses but finally hands the ball over. OMAR leads the way through the tents.

Scene 14

In the dim light of a single tent, MOHAMMED and FATIMA can be seen speaking quietly with a MAN. The MAN puts out his hand and

MOHAMMED and FATIMA look at each other. Finally FATIMA picks up a bag and gives it to him. The MAN pulls out the candlestick and nods. He returns it to the bag and gives FATIMA a wad of notes. He exits. MOHAMMED sits, his head between his hands. FATIMA covers her face with her hands and silently weeps. JAMAL enters.

Jamal Mum, what is it?

Fatima Nothing, Jamal, go to sleep while you can. We're leaving in a few hours.

> *FATIMA weeps.*

Jamal What's wrong?

Fatima I'm tired, son.

Jamal Why are you crying?

Fatima I'm sad too.

Jamal Mum, do you remember when Bibi wrapped her doll in some dough and Dad baked it and old Mrs Nazrim bit into the bread and tore the doll's head off?

Fatima I am beyond cheering.

Jamal What about when Abdullah's goat ate his dad's beard when he was asleep?

> *FATIMA begins to smile, but cries instead.*

You always laugh at that one.

Fatima How can I laugh when we've lost everything?

Jamal We'll come back one day and get it back.

Fatima No, we'll never come back.

Jamal No, I have a way to bring us back.

Fatima How will we survive the journey to Australia?

Jamal Australia! We're going to Australia? That's fantastic, they've got a soccer team in Australia.

Fatima We must take a plane to Indonesia first. How will we survive?

> *REFUGEES begin to fold up their tents and gather their bundles.*

> *MOHAMMED rises and wakes a sleeping BIBI.*

Mohammed It's time.

They pick up their bundles. JAMAL realises one bag in particular is missing.

Jamal Where's the candlestick?

FATIMA and MOHAMMED freeze. JAMAL realises the truth.

Oh no, you've sold it.

FATIMA and MOHAMMED move to join the other REFUGEES who are slowly weaving in and out of the remaining tents.

We can't go. We're not protected anymore. We can't go.

The REFUGEES move as one group. JAMAL, finally resigned, joins them. They squeeze onto a platform. They lift their heads high. The roar of take-off is deafening.

Scene 15

A large group of extremely tired REFUGEES stands on a dock. They look out towards the audience/sea. Jamal's family stands in the centre. They are all absolutely still and stare out in amazement. They cannot take their eyes off the sight before them.

Bibi Dad, which boat is ours?
Mohammed I'm not sure, Bibi, one of them.
Bibi How will we all fit on two boats?
Mohammed I'm not sure, Bibi. It'll be fine.
Jamal But there are so many of us.
Mohammed I am sure no one will be left behind.
Jamal They're very small.
Mohammed They're fishing boats.

Silence. The people stare anxiously at the boats.

Bibi When can we get on our boat?
Fatima Be patient a bit longer, Bibi.
Bibi I'm tired of Indonesia.
Jamal I'm tired of waiting.
Mohammed Waiting is very tiring.

Fatima We will go soon.

Jamal When?

Fatima Soon.

Bibi But when?

Mohammed Soon.

They continue to look out. FATIMA talks quietly with MOHAMMED.

Fatima Mohammed, I don't think I can board that boat.

Mohammed I'm afraid we have no choice.

Fatima We're desert people. The sea is full of treachery.

Mohammed Think of it as hills of sand, rippling out across the land. We'll ride it, like we're riding a camel…

Fatima When did you last ride a camel?

OMAR, ball in hand, pushes through the children. They follow him.

Jamal Hey, that's my ball.

Omar Not anymore.

Jamal Give it to me, it's mine.

Bibi [*pushing back her head cloth*] Listen, donkey shit, that's Jamal's ball. His best friend, Yusuf, gave it to him when we left our village in Afghanistan.

Jamal You better hand it over, because when my sister takes off her head scarf it means she's pretty mad.

JAMAL makes a grab for the ball but OMAR hangs on. They both pull but they are evenly matched. Finally the ball drops. OMAR grabs at it.

Bibi No you don't.

BIBI pulls back her foot to kick the ball. In a stylised sequence, BIBI's movement slows as do the reactions of JAMAL and OMAR. BIBI gives an almighty kick and the ball disappears.

Jamal [*huge and elongated*] Nnnooooo!

They watch the flight of the ball as it soars out over the water. At the same time, the crowd of REFUGEES turns in one movement. MOHAMMED and FATIMA are pushed toward the front. They

35

move as if caught in a bottleneck. A SAILOR in yellow overalls is pushing people along to board the boat. He holds a long pole with a hook on the end.

Quick, Bibi, we're boarding the boat.

JAMAL grabs BIBI's hand and they go to the end of the crowd and try to push their way through.

Mum! Dad!

BIBI pulls away from JAMAL.

Bibi I'm going to get the ball.
Jamal Bibi, no.

BIBI runs to the edge of the dock, and lies on her stomach and looks for the ball. JAMAL comes after her.

Leave it. We'll lose Mum and Dad.

Bibi If we lose the ball, we won't get to do the plan. We won't get to be soccer stars and form a new government. We won't get to go home.

OMAR calls from a large tyre which lies against the dock. He has a stick in his hand.

Omar I'll get the soccer ball. We'll go halves.
Jamal Watch out, if the boat bumps into the dockside you'll be crushed.
Omar I'm okay. I've done a lot of fishing. I've nearly got it.

He begins to slip. He tries to regain his balance but disappears over the side. JAMAL calls to the departing crowd.

Jamal Help, there's a boy in the water.

JAMAL kneels down to peer into the water. BIBI runs to the SAILOR in the yellow overalls.

Bibi A boy has fallen into the water.

The SAILOR ignores her. BIBI shakes him.

You've got to help him. He's in the water.

BIBI grabs the pole. The SAILOR grabs it back and pushes BIBI aside. BIBI kicks him and he pushes her to the ground. BIBI bites him on the leg. The SAILOR roars with pain, bends down, picks BIBI up and flings her over his shoulder. He takes her to the side of the dock and is about to fling her into the water. JAMAL, distraught, stands.

Blackout.

Jamal [*voice-over*] Nnnooooo…

The lights come up on JAMAL, tightly spotlit. His arms are up as if he's falling.

Bibi, Bibi, Bibi, I can't see her, my eyes are stinging, it's so cold, so cold. Bubbles float around me in the gold shafts from the sun and grey shadows from the boat and pink stars from the smack on my head. The water's heavy, heavier than sand and I'm sinking. Look for Bibi. Shapes everywhere but no Bibi. Just shadows. Sinking. Sinking. Can't find Bibi. Close my eyes. Can't find her. Can't find her. I can see Australia. Green soccer pitches and goalposts of solid gold and little stools for one-legged goalies to sit on. Me and Bibi winning the Cup Final for Dubbo Abattoirs United.

His voice fades quietly as does the spotlight to black.

The lights come up on JAMAL who is on his hands and knees, spluttering. Another SAILOR unhooks a pole from JAMAL's back. A spluttering BIBI and OMAR, ball gripped tightly in his hands, sit up beside JAMAL.

JAMAL remembers his parents.

Mum. Dad.

Bibi [*pointing out to sea*] Look.

JAMAL follows her direction.

Jamal Oh, no.

The lights come up on FATIMA and MOHAMMED. They are dismayed. They hold each other and look out. They wave. They fade away.

[*Shouting*] Mum! Dad!
Bibi Come back. Please.

Scene 16

The REFUGEES sleep tightly cramped in rows. One person in a row turns over and the next follows. Suddenly one person sits up, holds their stomach and groans. He or she is joined by another, and then another. They are seasick.

OMAR, JAMAL and BIBI are in the front row. OMAR sits up and groans. He gets up quickly and goes to the side of the boat to be sick. Others, at various intervals, do the same. JAMAL and BIBI sit up sleepily. OMAR returns and sits between them.

Omar It'll get worse than this. When the waves get really big, you'll be chucking too.

He immediately goes to the side of the boat to vomit.

Jamal I feel fine.
Bibi Me too.
Jamal I think it's because we're used to rolling from side to side in Dad's taxi.

OMAR returns.

Omar You just wait, the boat will be like a drunken camel and your stomachs will be turning somersaults.

He stops abruptly and gets up to be sick.

Bibi I'm hungry, Jamal.
Jamal Not long now, Bibi.
Bibi You're not going to tell me to be patient again, are you?

The REFUGEES are standing up and forming a queue. The SAILOR in yellow overalls is dishing out soup from a large pot.

Jamal No, I don't have to. Look, soup.

They join the queue. The person in front of them is draped in a blanket from head to toe and is next in line for soup. BIBI accidentally stands on the blanket and it is pulled off to reveal a teenage girl, RASHIDA, wearing shorts and t-shirt with a sparkly pattern on the front. Her arms and legs are bare. Her hair is uncovered and sticks out in all directions. She wears make-up which includes green lipstick. She wears lace-up construction boots. JAMAL, BIBI and the SAILOR gawk at her.

The SAILOR drops the ladle into the soup. RASHIDA holds out a tin for her soup but the SAILOR scowls at her and waves her away. She tries again, but this time the SAILOR growls his contempt at her.

Sailor No soup.

RASHIDA holds out her tin once more.

I said, no soup.

She moves away, pulls the blanket around her and sits down. BIBI erupts.

Bibi That's not fair. That soup's for everyone. It's not yours. You can't decide who gets it. You mangy camel, you slimy snake, you—
Sailor [*pointing to BIBI*] No soup.
Bibi You—

JAMAL covers her mouth.

Jamal Soup, please.
Sailor No soup.

JAMAL pulls BIBI away and they sit back on the deck.

Jamal Bibi, you've got to stop.
Bibi What?
Jamal You go too far. You sneak out and play soccer when you know you're not allowed, you throw rocks at trucks, you kick and bite. You've got to learn to keep your mouth shut.
Bibi [*loudly*] I don't care, Jamal. I like to go far.

RASHIDA is sitting with her back to BIBI and JAMAL. She turns her head.

39

Rashida That lizard breath needs to be taught a lesson. Hi, I'm Rashida.

Pause. JAMAL is uncomfortable talking to this unusual girl. BIBI tries to follow his lead but can't help herself.

Bibi Rashida's a boy's name.

Rashida My parents liked the name. They didn't care if I was a girl. They're like that.

OMAR joins them and visibly reacts when he sees RASHIDA.

Omar I've never seen anything like her. Why is she dressed like that?

Rashida Because I'm not in Afghanistan now. I'm free to wear whatever I like. And to say whatever I like, so why don't you go away.

Jamal He's with us.

RASHIDA sneeringly looks OMAR up and down and then turns her back on them.

Scene 17

A SMUGGLER stands on a box to make an announcement. He holds a club in one hand and a tin bucket in another. He beats the club on the bucket to draw everyone's attention.

Smuggler To continue your journey to Australia each of you must pay another hundred dollars.

The REFUGEES sound their displeasure in one voice. The SMUGGLER furiously beats the bucket with his club and they are silent. OMAR, JAMAL and BIBI are afraid.

Pay the full price or we turn back.

This time the REFUGEES wail. Another smuggler, the SAILOR in yellow overalls, takes the bucket and collects money and valuables.

Omar [*in a tiny voice*] I haven't got anything.

Jamal Nor have I.

The SMUGGLER on the box continues.

Smuggler It's a long way to Australia, it's easy for us to turn back. You choose.

The SAILOR in yellow has come to the children. He shoves the bucket in JAMAL's face.

Sailor Pay up.

Jamal We haven't got anything.

Sailor Pay up.

JAMAL slowly lifts up the soccer ball as an offering. The SAILOR sneers.

Pay up.

RASHIDA suddenly stands and hands a watch to the SAILOR.

Rashida Four people.

He studies the watch and tosses it into the bucket. They wait to see if he is satisfied. He looks at them. OMAR silently prays, JAMAL holds on tight to a growling BIBI. Finally the SAILOR moves on. The children sigh with relief. RASHIDA sits as before, her back turned to them. For a moment they are uncertain what to do. Suddenly OMAR stands in front of her.

Omar [*stretching out his arms*] I want to hug you so much, Rashida.

Rashida Thanks, but no.

Omar I want to hug your father so much too.

They all laugh. The friendship is forged.

Bibi Thank you, Rashida.

Jamal Thank you, Rashida. My name is Jamal. This is Bibi.

Omar And I'm Omar. Where did you get such a valuable watch?

Rashida Dad bought it with the remainder of his savings. He knew this would happen.

JAMAL stares out at the horizon.

Jamal Mum. Mum, if you can possibly hear me, please, please give up your wedding ring without a fight.

Scene 18

A drone fills the silence. People are hungry and attempt to sing the hunger away.

BIBI and OMAR sit either side of JAMAL, looking out to sea. They nurse their stomachs.

Bibi I'm hungry.
Omar I'm hungry.
Bibi I'm hungry.
Omar I'm hungry.
Bibi I'm—
Jamal I know, you're hungry. What can I do?
Rashida Don't you have anything to eat?
Jamal No. Our parents have got everything and they're on the other boat.
Omar So are mine.
Rashida I have a can of sardines.

> *They stare at her enviously. She unzips a pink suitcase and mimes taking out a can of sardines. They groan with disappointment.*

It looks like any old can of sardines but it's not. In this can there are little fish that look like ordinary sardines but these sardines are special. They are magical. [*She pauses playfully.*] Here, there is one each.

> *They hold back for a moment and then pretend to take a sardine.*

Hold them by the tail. Lift your heads up so. [*She holds her sardine up over her mouth.*] Drop it into your mouth, but don't be startled because it will feel very strange. It will immediately feel much bigger, more plump. Quickly swallow it down because it will grow very quickly and soon it will be too large to go down your throat. Now swallow.

They all swallow their fish.

Feel it in your belly. Feel how big it gets. Oh, I couldn't fit anything more if I tried. I am so full. Do you feel it? Are your bellies full?

She smiles at them and they laugh with her.

Bibi I think I'm going to split open.

Jamal It hurts, I'm so full.

Omar I don't think I'll ever have to eat again.

RASHIDA's suitcase is open and JAMAL sees something in it.

Jamal [*pointing into the case*] Rashida, is that what I think it is?

RASHIDA pulls out a big plastic bag of flour.

Rashida This?

Jamal Rashida, not only are your sardines magic, but you have more magic in that bag than you could ever imagine.

Rashida I have?

Omar She has?

Bibi Has she?

Jamal Right now, what's in that bag is more precious than gold, or season tickets for Manchester United.

Rashida Wow. [*She picks up the flour and holds it as if it's very valuable.*] Here. Take it, wield your magic. All I hope is that it makes something to eat.

JAMAL takes the flour and bows reverently.

Scene 19

It is the middle of the night. Two SMUGGLERS hold torches on some flat bread which has been laid on the engine to cook.

Smuggler 1 Hurry up.

Smuggler 2 This better be worth it.

Jamal Give me some light. I can't see what I'm doing.

They shine their torches on JAMAL while he kneads dough in a plastic bucket. He has flour on the end of his nose.

I might have put in too much salt. Had to guess how much seawater would do the trick. And a plastic bucket isn't the best way to get the stretchiness right.

The SMUGGLERS shine their light back on the flat bread.

Hey! I need some light.

The torches return to him.

It's not ready yet. Smell it. Mmm, smell it. There is no other smell like it. Especially when you're as hungry as I am. The engine is just hot enough. Lucky Rashida's parents sent her off with a bag of flour. And lucky that I come from a long line of bakers. [*He looks down in the dark toward his feet.*] What's this water? My feet are wet. Our boat isn't leaking, is it?

The torches return to the bread.

The boat isn't leaking, is it? Is it? Is it?

Both SMUGGLERS grab at the bread and it tears in two. The torches go out. JAMAL calls out from the darkness.

Hey!

Scene 20

RASHIDA and OMAR are eating bread hungrily.

Omar Your brother's a genius.

Rashida Smarter than Einstein.

BIBI, feeling seasick, pulls away from the sight of the bread.

Omar I could be a genius too if these dumb fish would bite.

He drags up a fishing line.

Rashida You have to have bait on your hook, Omar. How many times do I have to explain?

JAMAL staggers through the people to join his friends. He holds his belly and is groaning.

Omar Have some of your delicious bread, Jamal.

Jamal Please, don't mention food ever again.

Rashida I read somewhere that seasickness is meant to wear off after a day.

Omar A week, more like. Only five days to go, Jamal.

JAMAL groans.

Rashida Here.

She pulls out a spare t-shirt from her case and knots it around JAMAL's head.

It'll keep the sun off.

Omar What about me?

RASHIDA pulls out spare shorts this time and pulls them right over OMAR's head. They laugh. OMAR pulls them up and gives a cheeky grin.

Jamal [*ironically*] Remind me why we're doing this.

Bibi We're going to Australia.

Jamal Why?

Bibi To find our mum and dad.

Omar Because life in Australia is good.

Jamal That's right. I forgot. People laugh all the time in Australia, even in their sleep they laugh.

Bibi What's so funny?

Omar Everything. Apparently you can't stop. You are just so unbelievably happy.

Bibi That sounds like a good place.

Rashida We'll never be afraid in Australia. Only if we stand on a snake or meet a crocodile.

Bibi They have so much food they eat out of buckets. Don't they, Jamal?

Jamal And they have a world champion soccer team—Dubbo Abattoirs United.

Omar I am looking forward to it.
Jamal So am I, Omar. So am I.

BIBI groans and RASHIDA props her head on her knee.

Rashida You'll be all right, Bibi. You'll be all right.
Bibi [*wistfully*] I like your hair, Rashida.
Rashida Thanks, Bibi.
Bibi And I like your green lips.
Rashida Thanks.
Bibi I even like your big boots.
Rashida They're cool, aren't they?
Bibi Rashida?
Rashida Yes, Bibi.
Bibi Do you think you'll ever wear a veil again?
Rashida Never. I only wore it when I left the house. And only then because I was forced to. I wore these sort of clothes under my veil anyway. My mother sometimes wears her bikini.
Bibi How many days have we been on this boat?
Jamal Five, I think.
Rashida Six.
Bibi How many days until we get to Australia?
Jamal Three days. Three long days. Best forget what day it is.
Bibi I don't want to forget what day it is. It's my birthday.

JAMAL frantically calculates the date.

Jamal She's right. Oh, Bibi, I'm sorry.
Omar How could you have forgotten?
Rashida It's bad enough being stuck out here in the middle of the ocean on your birthday but to have your family forget is terrible.
Jamal I know. I know. Happy birthday, Bibi.
Rashida & Omar [*together*] Happy birthday, Bibi.
Jamal Let's plan a party for your birthday. We'll have it in Australia.
Bibi [*brightening*] Okay.
Omar My birthday's in four months.

RASHIDA elbows OMAR.

Rashida But it's not today.

Jamal In Australia, when it's your birthday, the Australian government comes round to your house with a cake and fizzy drinks.

Bibi Is this true?

Jamal [*hesitating*] It could be true, a good government would quite likely do something like that.

Omar And would they bring sardines?

Jamal Yes, probably.

Rashida And hamburgers with onion and egg and chilli sauce?

Jamal Definitely.

Omar Brilliant. What's a hamburger?

Bibi I prefer ice-cream.

Rashida It's your birthday; you can have anything you want.

Jamal In Australian supermarkets, they sell fifty different kinds of ice-cream.

Omar Fifty? What's a supermarket?

Rashida It doesn't have stalls like a normal market. It's one big shop that sells everything.

OMAR picks up his fishing line.

Omar Even bait?

Rashida Everything. My mum loved supermarkets.

Jamal Your mum?

Rashida I was born in Australia. When I was still a baby, we went back to Afghanistan to care for my grandparents. When they died the government refused to let us return to Australia. My parents are very sad. They love Australia. And they love me, they only had enough money for me to get out.

She looks out sadly to sea as she thinks of her parents.

Jamal Bibi, I will buy you a birthday gift when we get to Australia. At the supermarket. What would you like it to be?

Bibi Anything at all?

Jamal Anything.

Bibi I would like my own soccer ball.

They smile at each other. The four children snuggle down to sleep.

Scene 21

The boat is quiet and everyone rests. JAMAL stands and looks out to sea curiously.

Jamal There's a boat coming towards us.

> *BIBI stands and looks out with JAMAL.*

Bibi Is it Mum and Dad? Have we caught up with them?

> *They both look out eagerly for a moment.*

Jamal No, it's too big to be Mum and Dad's boat.

> *OMAR and RASHIDA get up sleepily and join them. OMAR waves tentatively.*

Omar Who are they?
Jamal I don't know.
Rashida Perhaps they've brought food and water.
Bibi Who are they?
Omar They're wearing tracksuits and trainers.
Jamal They couldn't be a soccer team, could they?
Bibi No, Jamal, no.

> *The entire boatload of REFUGEES has by now woken and got to their feet, totally focused on the arrival of this boat.*

Rashida Who are they?
Jamal They're carrying automatic weapons.

> *A beat. The people in one voice finally recognise who they are.*

Refugees Pirates.
Rashida *[in a small voice]* Oh, no.

> *A platform carrying a band of men with rifles, moves slowly forward. They are silhouetted against a vast sky.*

> *The SAILOR in yellow, bucket of loot in his hand, jumps across to the now close platform. He raises the bucket jubilantly.*

A chorus of whispers from the REFUGEES sounds.

Refugees They're abandoning us. They're abandoning us.

A GIRL's high-pitched scream cuts through the whispering.

Rashida [*in a small voice*] Oh, no.

A spotlight captures a frantic young GIRL struggling madly between two PIRATES as she is taken onto the platform.

The four children are in shock.

Jamal They're taking the girls. [*Moving into action*] Quick.

He takes the knotted t-shirt off his head and pulls BIBI's head scarf off and puts the t-shirt on her head instead.

Bibi, do something with your skirt.

BIBI pulls her skirt through her legs to make trousers.

Jamal Omar, quickly, give Rashida your hat.
Omar I haven't got a hat.

He remembers the shorts on his head and gives them to RASHIDA.

Jamal Put them on. Tuck your hair up.

He wraps the blanket around RASHIDA and smears her make-up over her face. He pushes the girls down.

Don't move.

He checks on the PIRATES who are making their way through the REFUGEES.

Keep your heads down.

They lower their heads.

Don't say a word. Not a word.

They nod.

A PIRATE comes and looks them up and down. Suspicious, he bends and looks closely at RASHIDA.

49

To divert him, JAMAL picks up the soccer ball and holds it in the air. He calls to the PIRATE.

Hey! I'm going to be number one striker for Afghanistan.

The PIRATE ignores him.

Hey!

He throws the ball at the PIRATE and hits him on the head. The PIRATE rises and fixes JAMAL with a stare. JAMAL has retrieved the ball and holds it now with his foot.

You're useless. Come on, see if you can take it from me.

He does some fancy footwork. The PIRATE suddenly lunges at JAMAL and knocks him to the ground. JAMAL quickly gets up, picks up the ball and throws it at the PIRATE who is looking at RASHIDA again. The PIRATE is diverted once more. He knocks JAMAL down and kicks him, extremely hard. JAMAL screams in pain.

The lights fade to black to the accompaniment of thirty hands thunderously drumming the deck.

The drumming hands reach a crescendo as the lights come up on JAMAL.

I'm Dubbo Abattoirs United and I've got the ball. Everything is good. The sun is shining. The grass is green. The goalposts are solid gold. Mum and Dad are among the spectators, smiling and waving. My hip hurts but it doesn't stop me dazzling the Cup Final crowd with my footwork.

He is interrupted by BIBI giving an almighty scream which resounds from the darkness.

What is it, Bibi? There's no army truck on the pitch. No soldiers with guns. No women running for their lives. Please, Bibi, everything is good here.

BIBI screams again.

Stop it, Bibi, you'll wake me and I'm about to score a goal. Look at those goalposts. They are waiting for this ball to soar between them.

The lights come up on BIBI.

Bibi Jamal!

JAMAL wakes but is still sluggish. He looks down.

Jamal What's this?

Bibi Wake up, Jamal. We're sinking.

Jamal But, Bibi, my goal.

Bibi Jamal, wake up!

JAMAL comes out of his sleep entirely.

Jamal We're sinking.

Blackout.

Scene 22

The REFUGEES form a long line and rhythmically bail water. The movement is mesmerising. There's desperation to it but it is also a powerful show of determination.

The lights come up on BIBI and JAMAL who have tied themselves together and are also bailing water.

Bibi This boat is going to sink.

Jamal No, keep bailing.

Bibi But the water—

Jamal It's working.

Bibi It's rising.

Jamal Keep bailing.

Bibi This is hopeless.

Jamal Remember the secret of soccer. Never give up, even when things are looking—

Bibi All right! Don't say hopeless. I can say hopeless but you can't. If you say hopeless then it really will be hopeless.

Jamal Keep scooping, then.

Bibi You keep scooping, then.

Jamal And don't stop.

Bibi And don't you stop.

Jamal Never.
Bibi Never.
Jamal Because we come from a long line of bakers.
Bibi And bakers never stop.
Jamal Up at three o'clock in the morning.
Bibi Every morning.
Jamal Dragging sacks of flour.
Bibi Kneading dough.
Jamal Reaching into scalding ovens.
Bibi Making loaf…
Jamal After loaf…
Bibi After loaf.
Jamal They never stop.

> *Behind BIBI and JAMAL, the other REFUGEES begin to stop bailing. One by one they stand up and look out. They look terrified. At last BIBI stops and stands. JAMAL remains furiously bailing.*

And I'm not going to stop. And nor are you.
Bibi Jamal, look.

> *JAMAL continues to bail.*

Jamal Keep bailing, Bibi. Keep bailing.
Bibi It's a warship. It's got guns longer than our boat.

> *A MAN picks up his small CHILD and holds her desperately up in the air.*

Man Don't shoot. There are children on board.

> *A WOMAN holds her BABY up in the air.*

Woman There are women and babies, please don't hurt us.

> *Another MAN moves forward hopefully.*

Man It's an Australian ship.
All Australian.
Man It is. It's Australian.

> *They cheer. BIBI drops down beside JAMAL.*

Bibi Jamal, you can stop, it's an Australian ship. Jamal, stop, Australia has come to get us. We've been saved.

Finally JAMAL stops bailing and looks up. He and BIBI stand in shock.

Man Get your things.

People eagerly gather their bundles.

Woman Hand them my baby.
Man It's a miracle.
Woman We would have sunk.
Man It's as if they knew.

Everyone waits. Their smiles gradually fade. A MAN steps forward.

Man We're sinking. We need to board your ship and quick.

Beat.

Refugee What are they waiting for?
Woman Help us, we're sinking, the water is rising very fast.

Beat.

Refugee What are they waiting for?
Man Save the women and children at least.

Beat.

All What are they waiting for?

Others join in.

Others Help us. Help us. Help us. We're refugees.

Silence. Again they wait.

Bibi [*to JAMAL*] What are they waiting for, Jamal?
Jamal I don't know, Bibi.

They wait. The light dims.

Scene 23

In a dimly lit cabin, ANDREW, a serviceman, stands in the doorway holding a tray in his hands, looking in on two children sleeping on camp beds.

Andrew [*whispering*] Are you two asleep?

> *JAMAL sits up on his elbow.*

I've got some more for you to eat if you're hungry.

> *He offers the tray to JAMAL who nods.*

I didn't know if you'd remember me. You might remember my ears. They definitely remember you and your sister. You held onto them pretty tight when I carried you aboard. Very good handles, my ears.

> *He laughs and put down the tray. He checks the sleeping BIBI's forehead.*

Good, she's sleeping peacefully.

> *JAMAL speaks but ANDREW cannot hear him.*

Jamal I wish I knew how to ask him about my mother and father.

Andrew When you're ready, there's another serve of fish fingers, chips and peas here for you. And a serve for your sister when she wakes up.

Jamal If only I could ask you if my mum and dad are safe.

> *ANDREW is reluctant to leave. He is biding his time because he has something to say.*

Andrew And there's more when you've finished that lot. What about some ice-cream? Can I get you some ice-cream? Maybe later. You take it easy. You and your sister sleep all you want. I'll leave you alone then, unless there's something else I can get you.

Jamal Do you know if my mother and father are waiting for us in Australia?

Andrew How's your hip? It'd hurt, a bruise that big. When I was a kid I was hit by a truck and I didn't have a bruise as big as the one you've got. [*Pause.*] Do you need another pillow?

He offers JAMAL a pillow. JAMAL declines.

I guess I'll get out of your hair. I'll be on my way.

Finally ANDREW gets to the door. He steps out and immediately steps back in.

You're right, then? Good. Good on you.

He freezes at the door, before turning to face JAMAL squarely.

You probably don't understand a word I'm saying, but I want to tell you how sorry I am. [*Pause.*] We took so long. We saw you and all I wanted to do was dive in and come and get you but … [*Pause.*] We should have come straight away, but there was … paperwork. We had to wait, we didn't want to, but we had to wait for the paperwork to come through. [*He looks at his feet.*] I'll leave you to your fish fingers.

JAMAL looks a bit puzzled but he waves and ANDREW finally exits. He puts his plate on his lap.

Jamal As soon as I can I am going to send you some fish fingers, Yusuf. They are truly magnificent.

OMAR comes to the door.

Omar You can get a gut-ache eating too many chips. I know because I ate a thousand of them.

Jamal [*gleefully*] Omar! Where's Rashida?

Omar She's a bit dehydrated but she's okay. And so is our other good friend.

Jamal Who?

OMAR reveals the soccer ball from behind his back and JAMAL cheers.

Scene 24

A line-up of REFUGEES with JAMAL, BIBI, RASHIDA and OMAR holding each other's outstretched hands. They wear huge smiles.

Bibi Do you believe it?
Jamal No.
Rashida That's because it's still moving.
Omar Will it ever stop?
Bibi Perhaps this is what Australia feels like.
Rashida Let's try to stop it. We'll teach our bodies that we have truly arrived on land. On the count of three, jump. One, two, three.

> *They jump.*

Clockwise from top left: Ashwin Gore as Jamal, Andrew Gray (Ensemble), Bella Partridge (Ensemble), Emily Edmondson as Bibi and Paul Hee (Ensemble) in the 2005 atyp production. (Photo: Giselle Haber)

Omar I'm still swaying.

Bibi And me.

Jamal At least we won't get seasick on land.

Rashida It'll wear off in a day or two.

Omar We are definitely here, aren't we?

Jamal In Australia.

Bibi In Australia.

Omar We're in …

Rashida Australia.

Jamal We're walking on Australian dirt.

Rashida Australian grass.

Bibi That's an Australian ant.

Omar These are Australian flies on my face.

Bibi We made it.

Jamal Let's explore. We'll go find all the places we've heard about.

Omar A shopping centre with a fountain.

Bibi Can we dip our feet into it?

Jamal What about the cinema with fourteen movies showing at once.

Omar Fourteen!

Bibi I would like to see all fourteen.

Jamal Let's go and find an Australian supermarket.

Rashida Where you can buy anything you want.

Omar If you've got money.

Bibi This time we'll just look.

Omar Let's go.

Jamal Okay.

Rashida Let's go.

Bibi Okay.

They remain motionless. They look out and their smiles fade.

Rashida [*quietly*] They will find them.

Jamal I thought they would be here.

Bibi Me too.

Jamal When we got closer to the jetty I thought I saw them.

Bibi Me too.

Rashida The ship will find them and bring them here soon. [*Pause.*] And your parents too, Omar.

> *OMAR bows his head.*

Bibi They will, won't they, Jamal? They'll find them and bring them to us?

Jamal Yes, Bibi, they'll find them.

> *JAMAL hugs BIBI. He tries to cheer her up.*

Bibi When Mum and Dad get here we'll do all those things.

Scene 25

JAMAL, BIBI, RASHIDA and OMAR burst into action. They line up ready for the soccer match to begin. A crowd of people on the sidelines cheers them on.

Bibi Refugees versus Aussies. We're going to kick ass ...
Jamal [*laughing*] Bibi! Where did you pick that up from?

> *They take on postures anticipating a pass of the soccer ball while JAMAL narrates the game.*

Bibi kicks the ball to me.
Rashida Good pass.
Jamal I sidestep a tackle from an Australian sailor and pass to Omar. He shoots.

> *The supporters cheer from the sidelines.*

A bit hopeful from forty metres out. The goalkeeper runs out and picks up the ball where it stopped.
Bibi [*exuberant*] I'm having a great time.
Rashida Me too.
Jamal It's wonderful to have all the people from our boat here.

> *They cheer. JAMAL notices that OMAR is looking very gloomy.*

Don't worry, Omar, you'll get better with practice.
Omar Have you heard what people are saying?
Jamal Don't worry about them, they probably can't even kick a ball.

Omar Not that, what they're saying about this camp.

Jamal The Aussies score again. Six nil. We've got to come up with something good.

Bibi I'm ready for it.

Rashida Bring it on.

Omar Jamal, are you listening to me?

Jamal No. I'm not. If you want to win at soccer you've got to concentrate on the game.

Omar They are saying that this is not where we think it is.

Jamal You don't see Manchester United gossiping during matches.

Rashida Jamal, Bibi, run up their end and I'll try and get the ball to you.

Jamal She means play deep striker.

Omar They're saying this isn't Australia.

Jamal [*overlapping* OMAR] Bibi's off like a rocket. I can hardly keep up with her. Not only can she kick harder than me, she can run faster. I'll have to train hard or she might get a place with Dubbo Abattoirs United and I won't.

Rashida Jamal!

Jamal Oh, wow. Rashida's done it. The ball's flying towards me. I trap it on my chest and turn towards goal. My hip hurts but I can't worry about that.

Bibi Watch out, Jamal.

Jamal Two Aussie defenders on me. I saw David Beckham do this once. Two defenders, go between them, get them confused.

> *The crowd cheers.*

I pass to Bibi, who's in a great shooting position. Do a scud shot, Bibi.

Bibi I'm blocked.

Jamal She passes back to me. The two Aussie defenders thunder towards me.

Omar Pass!

Bibi Shoot!

> *They freeze.*

Jamal I hesitate. Then shoot. The goalie doesn't even move. The ball's like a missile, flashing between the posts, over the crowd and slamming into the compound fence.

JAMAL flings his arms into the air.

Bibi [*joyfully*] Goal.

JAMAL, with arms still high in the air, stops and waits for the cheering. There's none. The crowd looks stunned. JAMAL is confused for a moment.

Jamal Was I offside?

Bibi No, it was definitely a goal.

The silence is shattered by a chilling and heartrending wailing. Some people fall to their knees with grief. Others hug each other. JAMAL, his arms still in the air, is afraid. A MAN steps forward.

Man The other boat. [*Pause.*] It's sunk.

Silence. Slowly and pitifully, JAMAL lets his arms drop. Blackout.

Scene 26

BIBI and JAMAL sit cross-legged facing each other, their heads drop forward and touch.

'Caravan Song', from 'Inside Afghanistan', a recording by Deben Bhattacharya.

RASHIDA enters.

Rashida The warship is doing everything it can. They've picked up three young survivors. And they're still looking. [*She puts down the tray and lifts up a deflated soccer ball.*] Here's your soccer ball. When you scored your beautiful goal, it got punctured on the barbed wire. [*She takes a deep breath.*] Jamal and Bibi, you've still got me. I know it's not the same, but we're family.

RASHIDA looks at the grieving boy and girl.

I'm so sorry.

> *BIBI and JAMAL remain still. RASHIDA exits.*

Scene 27

It is night and the moon shines brightly over the soccer pitch. JAMAL lies face up, spreadeagled in the middle of the pitch. From somewhere out of the darkness someone is weeping. JAMAL sits up and listens. He stands.

Jamal Omar?

> *The lights come up on OMAR sitting on the side of the pitch. He is sobbing into his hands. JAMAL goes to him.*

Omar, I'm so sorry. You've lost your parents too.

Omar I've something to tell you.

Jamal No more bad news I hope.

Omar My parents weren't on the boat.

Jamal What?

Omar They died when I was two.

> *Pause.*

Jamal How did you get a ticket to Australia?

Omar I didn't. I hung around a big family in the camp and when they got on buses so did I. People thought I was with them.

Jamal What about the plane?

Omar Same thing. I lied to you.

> *JAMAL looks at OMAR in silence.*

Jamal Bibi and I have a lot to learn from you. You have no parents but it hasn't held you back. Look at you, you're here, you've made it, across the world, all the way to Australia.

Omar But it's not true.

Jamal I don't care what you say. Like you, I'll learn to look after myself. And Bibi too.

Omar No, Jamal, it's not true that we're in Australia. We're not.

Jamal What? Where else could we be?

Omar We're on an island quite a distance from Australia.

Jamal On an island? Why have they brought us to an island?

Omar They don't want us.

Jamal Why wouldn't they want us? We've done nothing wrong.

Omar They won't take us.

Jamal They'll take us all.

Omar They'll send us back.

Jamal To our deaths? How could they send us back?

Omar I come from a long line of thieves. They won't take me.

Jamal And I come from desert warriors and bakers. They won't care.

Omar If we get to Australia they will put us in prison. There's talk in the camp. There are prisons with wire in the middle of a desert.

Jamal We're kids. The Australian government looks after children.

Omar How do you know, Jamal?

Jamal Because Australians are kind.

Omar Are you sure?

Jamal I'm absolutely certain.

Omar Which one are you? Baker or warrior?

JAMAL thinks for a moment.

Jamal I'm a bit of both.

Scene 28

JAMAL is in a tent. He is weeping. BIBI puts her head inside the tent.

Bibi Jamal, quick, come outside.

Jamal No, I want to stay here.

Bibi Come on, people are going down to the jetty.

Jamal I don't want to go.

Bibi The warship is back. It's sitting in the harbour.

Jamal I'm not interested.

Bibi There's a rubber boat coming in to shore.

Jamal Bibi, you know Mum and Dad aren't coming back, don't you?

Bibi They're bringing in the survivors. Maybe they saw Mum and Dad before—

Jamal You go, I don't want to.

Bibi They might have a message for us.

Jamal Tell me later if they do.

Bibi It's not hopeless, Jamal. Remember? It's not hopeless.

She pulls the flaps of the tent down and exits.

JAMAL hugs himself miserably.

After a few moments BIBI calls from the other side of the tent. Her voice is small and tremulous.

Jamal, Jamal, Jamal.

Jamal Leave me alone, Bibi.

She calls to JAMAL again, a joyous call.

Bibi Jamal!

Jamal [*angrily*] Do you hear me, Bibi, go away! I mean it, I want you to leave me alone.

There is no response. JAMAL listens. He stands and slowly, tentatively, moves to the entrance of the tent. He opens the flaps of the tent and steps outside.

The lights come up on FATIMA and MOHAMMED with BIBI between them. JAMAL stands as if transfixed, unable to move.

Mum? Dad?

FATIMA and MOHAMMED fade. BIBI cries miserably. JAMAL takes her in his arms.

Scene 29

ANDREW holds Jamal's soccer ball. It is mended with an Australian flag patch. JAMAL enters. They speak, but neither understands the other.

Andrew Jamal. Here, I mended it for you.

JAMAL takes the ball. He is silent. He stares at ANDREW.

What is it? Is something wrong, Jamal?

JAMAL speaks but ANDREW cannot understand him.

Jamal All I want to know is why we're here and not in Australia?

Andrew I wish I knew how to explain to you—the Australian government changed its refugee policy.

Jamal I want to know why Australians don't want us.

Andrew The Australian government thought they'd get more votes by keeping you out. And they did.

Jamal Why don't Australians want us?

ANDREW drops his head. He shrugs.

Why?

Andrew I don't know.

JAMAL throws the soccer ball high into the air. It drops and he stops it with his foot. The scene dissolves behind him.

Scene 30

JAMAL does some fancy footwork with the ball.

Jamal The secret of soccer is to never give up, even when things are looking hopeless.

BIBI joins him.

Bibi Don't say hopeless.

Jamal We will reach Australia.

Bibi We will.

FATIMA and MOHAMMED join them to be followed by other REFUGEES.

Jamal And when we reach Australia life will be good.

Bibi It will.

Pause.

Jamal It will.

THE END

Young Adult plays
from Currency Press

Angela Betzien
THE HANGING
Three teenage schoolgirls go missing in Melbourne's hinterland. The clock is ticking, the search is on. One of the girls turns up days later. Confused and unkempt, she has no apparent memory of what happened and where her friends are. Sound familiar? *The Hanging* is a gripping thriller that questions the spectre of the missing girl in the Australian bush. Its mystery is a postmodern study of social panic and what lies hidden, just out of reach.
2F, 1M   *978-1-76062-050-9 PB, ebook also available*

CHILDREN OF THE BLACK SKIRT
A gothic fairytale. Three lost children discover an abandoned orphanage in the bush and learn a history of Australia through the spirits of children who have lived there, from convict times, through to World War II, the Stolen Generations and beyond.
14M, 12F (doubling possible)   *978-0-86819-760-9 PB, ebook also available*

HOODS
Exploring poverty and family violence, *Hoods* is a suburban tale of survival and solidarity against the odds. Winner of the Richard Wherrett Award and the AWGIE Award for Theatre for Young Audiences (2007).
1M, 1F   *978-0-86819-800-2 PB, ebook also available*

Felicity Castagna
THE INCREDIBLE HERE AND NOW
Adapted from the novel
Charcoal chicken, a white Pontiac Trans Am, the Council pool. Michael is living in the shadow of his older brother Dom. *The Incredible Here and Now* is a poignant rollercoaster ride celebrating life, first love, family and new beginnings, traversing the streets of Western Sydney.
7F, 6M (doubling possible)   *978-1-76062-133-9 PB*

Jack Davis
HONEY SPOT
The friendship between an Aboriginal boy and a white girl raises issues of race in a touching story of two families who seem to have nothing in common… until danger strikes, forcing them to face their prejudices.
3M, 2F   *978-0-86819-163-8 PB, ebook also available*

Eva di Cesare, Sandra Eldridge & Tim McGarry
HITLER'S DAUGHTER
Adapted from Jackie French's novel
Did Hitler have a daughter? And if he did, what happened to her? A tautly-written tale of suspense with a deeply human heart.
6M, 8F (doubling possible)   *978-0-86819-813-2 PB, ebook also available*

Nick Enright
BLACKROCK
It's Toby Ackland's birthday party down near the surf club—and that should mean heaps of grog, drugs and fun. But by the morning a young girl is dead. Who is responsible? Winner of the AWGIE Award for Stage (1996).
6M, 5F   *978-0-86819-477-6 PB, ebook also available*

Mary Morris
TWO WEEKS WITH THE QUEEN
Adapted from Morris Gleitzman's novel
Colin has a mission. He wants to speak to the Queen about his brother Luke who has cancer. Colin takes the lock off the back door and heads out alone. This play brilliantly combines comedy and tragedy to tell a tale of hope, courage and innocence.
4M, 2F   *978-0-86819-401-1 PB, ebook also available*

Kate Mulvany

JASPER JONES
Adapted from the novel by Craig Silvey
Charlie's 14 and smart. But when 16-year-old, constantly-in-trouble Jasper Jones appears at his window one night, Charlie's out of his depth. *Jasper Jones* interweaves the lives of complex individuals all struggling to find happiness among the buried secrets of a small rural community.
9M, 4F (doubling possible)   978-1-76062-004-2 PB, *ebook also available*

Debra Oswald

STORIES IN THE DARK
A terrified 12-year-old boy finds himself separated from his family in the unfamiliar streets of a war torn city. Into his life steps Anna, and so begins a journey into the world of ogres, princes, singing bones, foolish lads and wolf-mothers. Winner of the NSW Premier's Literary Award for Playwriting and the AWGIE Award for Young Audiences (2008).
32M, 23F (doubling possible)   978-0-86819-831-6 PB, *, ebook also available*

Lachlan Philpott

MICHAEL SWORDFISH
What would happen if someone you knew disappeared? How would you react? But who is Michael Swordfish? And who knows where he's gone? This play traverses the tumultuous landscape of the teenage experience with a sober truth and darkly comic voice. Winner of the AWGIE for Youth and Community Theatre (2017).
9M   978-1-76062-083-7 PB, *ebook also available*

SILENT DISCO
Tamara and Jasyn are in love. In a world of absent mothers and missing fathers, one teacher battles to keep another year of students out of the ranks of the vanished. Winner of Griffin Award (2009) & AWGIE Award for Stage (2012).
5F, 4M (doubling possible)   978-0-86819-961-0 PB, *ebook also available*

Sean Riley

BEAUTIFUL WORDS

An epic chronicle of refugee experiences, *Beautiful Words* weaves together three different stories of survival, told through the eyes of three children in different times and places. Winner of Jill Blewett Playwrights' Award (2004).
17M, 11F (doubling possible)   *978-0-86819-832-3 PB, ebook also available*

Ninna Tersman

PARASITES

Two teenagers fleeing unthinkable dangers find solace in each other amidst the damaging confines of an asylum seeker processing centre. This is the tender story of young people in a desperate situation, yearning for hope and home.
1F, 1M   *978-1-76062-053-0 PB, ebook also available*

Sandra Thibodeaux

MR TAKAHASHI (AND OTHER FALLING SECRETS)

Darwin, 1941. A town collapses under the threat of invasion. Mothers and daughters, sisters, friends, and entire cultures are torn apart by the secrets that start to fall. Is Mr Takahashi to blame? This play tells the stories of Darwin's multicultural and Indigenous women whose lives were forever changed by the bombings of February 19.
11F + chorus   *978-1-76062-008-0 PB, ebook also available*

Richard Tulloch

THE BOOK OF EVERYTHING

Adapted from Guus Kuijer's novel

Thomas sees things that other people ignore. Featuring Jesus, angels, and a girl with a leather leg, this is a magical story about a child learning in the face of fear and injustice.
4M, 5F   *978-0-86819-933-7 PB*

Alana Valentine

CYBERBILE / GROUNDED

Cyberbile is a candid, moving and sometimes shocking glimpse into the online world of today's teen generation. *Grounded* is about a young girl with a fascination for Newcastle's industrial port, exploring themes of isolation, belonging and disillusionment. Winner of three AWGIE Awards: Young Audiences, Major Award, and the Award for Playwriting (2013).

3F; 7M, 9F (doubling possible)   978-0-86819-984-9 *PB, ebook also available*

Matthew Whittet

GIRL ASLEEP

Caught in the headlights of her 15th birthday, Greta wishes she could be anywhere else. And strangely enough 'anywhere else' is exactly where she finds herself – a peculiar Through-the-Looking-Glass existence that transforms the weird hypocrisy of the adult world into something absurdly beautiful.

10F, 5M (doubling possible)   978-1-92500-572-1 *PB, ebook also available*